THE
BEAGLE

by Charlotte Wilcox

Content Consultant
Judith M. Musladin, M.D.
Education Chairman, Supporting Membership
National Beagle Club

CAPSTONE PRESS
MANKATO, MINNESOTA

C A P S T O N E   P R E S S
818 North Willow Street • Mankato, MN 56001
http://www.capstone-press.com

Library of Congress Cataloging-in-Publication Data
Wilcox, Charlotte.
    The beagle/by Charlotte Wilcox.
    p. cm.--(Learning about dogs)
    Includes bibliographical references (p. 46) and index.
    Summary: An introduction to the smallest member of the hound
family, which includes its history, development, uses, and care.
    ISBN 1-56065-539-9
    1. Beagles (Dogs)--Juvenile literature. [1. Beagles (Dogs) 2. Dogs.]
I. Title. II. Series: Wilcox, Charlotte. Learning about dogs.
SF429.B3W55 1998
636.753'7--dc21

                                                97-12208
                                                   CIP
                                                    AC

Photo credits
Mark Raycroft, 10, 12, 20, 38-39
Reynolds' Stock Photos, cover, 8, 14, 17
TwainHeart Beagles, 6, 28
Unicorn/Deneve Feigh, 25, 30; Robert Ginn, 26; Martha
    McBride, 32; John L. Ebling, 34
Faith A. Uridel, 4, 18, 22, 36, 40

Table of Contents

Quick Facts about the Beagle

Description

Height: Beagles stand 10 to 15 inches (25 to 38 centimeters) tall. Height is measured from the ground to the withers. The withers are the top of the shoulders.

Weight: Beagles weigh 15 to 25 pounds (seven to 11 kilograms).

Physical features: Beagles are small but muscular. They have brown eyes and long ears. They carry their tails high.

Color: Most beagles have black, white, and tan markings. Markings can also be cream, brown, or gray.

Development

Place of origin: Beagles came from England.

History of breed: Beagles descended from the hunting dogs of Europe.

Numbers: Almost 60,000 beagles are registered every year in the United States. Register means to record a dog's breeding records with an official club. About 1,500 are registered each year in Canada. Many more are not registered.

Uses

Most beagles in North America are family pets. Some are used as tracking dogs for law enforcement. A few beagles still hunt with their owners.

Chapter 1

A Snoopy Dog

In 1950, cartoonist Charles M. Schulz created the comic strip *Peanuts*. It is the story of Charlie Brown, his dog Snoopy, and their friends. Snoopy is a smart dog. He dreams of doing great things. When he decides to do something, he never gives up.

Snoopy became a national hero. People wrote books and made television shows about him. Stores sold Snoopy toys. A Snoopy theme park opened. Snoopy became North America's favorite beagle.

Snoopy is a good name for a beagle. Beagles are always sniffing around. They love to track the scent of a trail. When they are tracking a scent, they never give up.

Beagles are always sniffing around.

Beagles are the smallest members of the hound family.

The Smallest Hound

Beagles are the smallest members of the hound family. Hounds hunt in groups called packs. They find game hiding in woods or grass. Game is animals and birds that are hunted. A hound chases game out where hunters can shoot it.

In the past, different sizes of hounds were bred for hunting different sizes of game. Large hounds, such as greyhounds, hunted deer and bears. Medium-size hounds, such as foxhounds and coonhounds, hunted foxes and raccoons.

People needed smaller hounds for hunting rabbits and squirrels. These dogs could crawl through small spaces. They could chase game for hours. They needed good noses to follow winding trails. Small hounds were bred to have these qualities.

The small hounds were lovable pets. Hunters brought them in the house to play with their children. People called the small hounds beagles. The word beagle means small or of little value.

Despite their names, beagles are highly valued by those who own them. They are more than good hunters. They are smart and friendly. They make good pets.

Chapter 2
The Beginnings of the Breed

Ancient Greeks used small hounds more than 2,000 years ago. Packs of hounds chased small game out of the bushes. Hunters caught the game in nets.

Later, ancient Romans used packs of small hounds. The Romans brought their hounds when they conquered England and France. There, the Roman hounds were bred with local dogs. Different sizes of hounds developed.

The larger hounds ran fast. The hounds followed large game mostly by sight. They chased the game for hours until it became tired. Then hunters killed it with spears or arrows.

Small hounds are slower than larger hounds.

Beagles follow game mostly by scent.

Smaller hound breeds developed a keen sense of smell. They followed game mostly by scent. They chased the game into hunters' nets. They also chased game out of places hunters could not reach. Some hounds were trained to kill the game and bring it to the hunter.

Early Hound Stories

Some stories say that King Arthur and his Knights of the Round Table had small hounds. History records that Pwyll had a special breed of white hounds. Pwyll was an early Prince of Wales. His hounds were very good hunters.

In 1066, William the Conqueror became king of England. He was from France. He brought hounds from France to England. They were called Talbot hounds. They were large and mostly white. Like the English hounds, Talbots traced back to ancient Greek and Roman breeds.

Talbot hounds were bred with English dogs. The crosses produced the foxhound and the beagle. These two breeds look very much alike, but beagles are smaller. Both have markings of white with other colors. Both follow a trail by scent.

Chapter 3

The Development
of the Breed

Dogs were as important as weapons to early
hunters. People hunted large game with spears
or bows and arrows. They hunted smaller game
with slingshots. They also caught game in nets
and in snares. Hunters used dogs to find, chase,
corner, and sometimes kill game.

People started using guns for hunting more
than 500 years ago. Dogs were still important
to hunters. Hounds sniffed to find game in
bushes or tall grass. They chased game from
hiding places. They chased an animal out
where the hunter could shoot it.

Beagles chase game out of bushes and tall grass.

The Big Hunts

At one time in England, only the king was allowed to hunt deer. The king owned much of the land. He invited his friends on deer hunts. Packs of large hounds chased deer out of their hiding places.

Some of the king's family members and friends also owned land. They could not hunt deer unless they were invited by the king. So they hunted fox instead. The fox hunt became a popular sport.

Soon, all the rich men in England had kennels full of hounds. A kennel is a place where dogs are kept. The men met together for large hunts in the country. Hunters rode on horseback. They wore red coats. Each hunter brought his own pack of hounds to join the hunt.

Everyone rode out to an open field and let the dogs go. When the hounds found a fox, they began to bark. The fox would run with the hounds right behind. The chase was on.

It was a wild, noisy scene. When the fox was sighted, someone blew a horn. Hunters, horses, and hounds bounded across the fields.

Many English farmers once kept beagles for hunting.

The dogs kept up a constant wail. The horses' hooves pounded the earth. Everyone thought it was great fun.

But not everyone could afford to keep a stable full of horses and a kennel full of large hounds. Those who were not as wealthy also wanted to enjoy an exciting hunt. They could only afford small hounds. So they hunted rabbits.

Hounds that hunt rabbits need good noses.

Rabbit hunting requires a slower hound. This is because rabbit hunters usually hunt on foot. Hounds that hunt rabbits need good noses. A rabbit is not as easy to see as a fox or a deer. The dogs must find and follow the rabbit mostly by its scent.

Beagles had all the qualities needed for rabbit hunting. They were easy care for. They did not eat as much as the larger hounds. Almost everyone loved them.

Early Beagle Breeders

Many English farmers kept packs of beagles for hunting. Even kings and queens came to admire the small hounds. King Henry VIII raised beagles in the 1500s. They were called glove beagles because a person could hold one in a single hand.

Henry VIII's daughter was Queen Elizabeth I. She kept beagles. Her beagles were especially small. They were only about nine inches (23 centimeters) tall. They were called pocket beagles. People carried them in the pockets of their hunting coats.

Beagles in the United States

There were small hounds in the southern United States in the early 1800s. They were called beagles. But they were different from modern beagles. They were mostly white, and were different sizes.

The first true beagles came to North America in 1876. General Richard Rowett from Illinois brought several from England. He started the first beagle-breeding kennel. His hounds were a huge success. Beagles soon became popular in the eastern United States and Canada.

Chapter 4
The Beagle Today

Beagles are popular pets. They play with children as eagerly as they chase rabbits. They are clean and easy to keep in the house. Beagles live mostly in Europe, North America, South America, and Australia.

An Official Breed

Beagles became an official breed in the 1800s. In 1884, some beagle breeders from Philadelphia met. They started the first beagle club in North America. The American Kennel Club was formed the same year. Beagles were among the first dogs to be accepted as an official breed.

Now, the American Kennel Club registers almost 60,000 beagles every year. The Canadian Kennel Club registers about 1,500 per year.

The American Kennel Club registers almost 60,000 beagles every year.

Most beagles have white, black, and tan markings.

What Beagles Look Like

Beagles are small to medium in size. Their size is determined by their height. Height is measured from the ground to the withers.

There are two official beagle sizes in North America. Beagles measuring 13 inches (33 centimeters) or shorter are in the smaller class. Beagles measuring between 13 inches (33 centimeters) and 15 inches (38 centimeters) make up the larger class. Beagles cannot compete in official events if they are taller than 15 inches (38 centimeters).

Beagles have big, brown eyes and long, drooping ears. They often carry their tails up in the air. Their coats are thick and medium length.

Beagle Colors

Most beagles have black, white, and tan markings. The black markings often appear on the upper back. This is called a black blanket.

Markings can also be cream or different shades of brown. Some beagles have speckled gray. They are called blue beagles. Blue beagles often have light-colored eyes.

Most beagles' feet are white. The tips of their tails are also white.

A Musical Dog

Beagles like to use their musical voices. Hunters refer to the sound a hound makes as its note. Beagles bark or growl when something unfamiliar enters their territory. Their bark makes them sound bigger and meaner than they really are. Beagles seldom bite.

Besides barking and growling, beagles make two other special sounds. The sounds are baying and howling.

Several breeds of hounds make a baying sound. A bay is a long, singing bark. Hounds bay when they smell game.

Beagles howl when they corner an animal. The howl is a high-pitched wail. Beagles do not have to be out hunting to bay or howl. Sometimes beagles bay and howl for no clear reason.

Sometimes beagles bay and howl for no clear reason.

Chapter 5

The Beagle in Action

Beagles are happiest when they are busy. They like to go for walks and explore. Beagles also like to use their noses to hunt with people.

Beagle Field Trials

Today, people usually hunt with beagles for fun and show. Beagle clubs sponsor events called field trials. At a field trial, hunting dogs are judged on their ability to find and retrieve game. Beagles and their owners hunt rabbits. They usually let the rabbit go when the hunt is over.

Beagles like to go for walks.

Beagles often participate in field trials.

There are four types of field trials for beagles. They are the formal pack, brace, large pack, and small pack option.

The formal pack field trial is like the hunts in England centuries ago. Hunters wear green hunting coats, white pants or skirts, and black velvet caps. Hounds hunt in large packs. When the hounds smell a rabbit, they take off in chase. They bark and bay. Hunters use horns to direct the hounds. A hunt sometimes lasts all day.

In brace trials, two beagles work together. A rabbit is released and the beagles chase it. The dogs are judged mostly on their ability to track the rabbit by scent.

As many as 60 beagles compete in a large pack field trial. A large rabbit called a hare is the game. The pack tracks the hare in a group. These events are usually held in the midwestern and northeastern United States.

The small pack option is used to determine which dogs are afraid of guns. Beagles hunt in packs of at least six. No rabbits are released. The hounds must search for a wild rabbit. A gun is fired during the trial to see if a beagle will react. If one does, it is out of the competition.

The Beagle Brigade

The Beagle Brigade is a special group of beagles. They work for the U.S. Department of Agriculture. Their job is to find small amounts

of citrus fruit, beef, and pork coming into the country. These foods can carry pests and sicknesses.

Beagle Brigade dogs sniff suitcases and boxes at airports. They also sniff packages in post offices that get mail from other countries. They sniff for illegal substances.

Beagles were chosen for this work because of their good sense of smell. They also like people and are friendly. Because they are raised in packs, they do well in crowded, noisy places like airports.

Many beagles are working dogs. Some are used to find termites in buildings. A termite is an insect that eats wood. Termites can destroy buildings. Other beagles help people with emotional problems. Like many animals, beagles help some people show their feelings.

Beagles help some people show their feelings.

Chapter 6

Owning a Beagle

Beagles make good pets, but they are not for everyone. They were raised and used in packs for hundreds of years. They do not like to be alone. They need to be with people or other dogs most of the time.

Beagles do not get attached to one certain person. They love everyone in a family, especially children. They like to run, jump, and play. Beagles are always sniffing and exploring.

Beagles are friendly and happy. They are easy to get along with, but they are not always easy to train. This is because new sights, sounds, and smells grab their attention.

Beagles do not like to be alone.

A beagle needs a special place of its own.

Keeping a Beagle

Beagles do best living in a house with a family. They can live happily in a kennel as long as there are other dogs. Beagles should never be allowed to run free. They will follow their noses straight into trouble.

A beagle needs a special place of its own. Baskets, dog beds, and crates work well. If the place does not have a soft surface, it should be padded with an old blanket or pillow. Place it in a quiet corner away from drafts or direct heat. Outside, beagles need protection from rain, cold, heat, and wind.

Some people have their names and phone numbers put on their dog's collar. Some have a microchip implanted under the dog's skin. A microchip is a computer chip about the size of a grain of rice. When scanned, it shows the owner's name, address, and telephone number.

Feeding a Beagle

Kibble makes the best diet for many beagles. Kibble is dry dog food. It is inexpensive and easy to keep. Beagles are not big eaters. It is best to buy kibble in small amounts. Then it will always be fresh.

Most adult beagles can eat kibble straight from the bag. It is crunchy, so it helps keep their teeth clean. Kibble can also be moistened with water.

An average full-grown beagle eats six to eight ounces (168 to 224 grams) of kibble a day. Most people divide the food into two meals. A beagle should not be fed more than it needs. It is unhealthy for a dog to become overweight.

Dogs need plenty of water. They should always have clean water to drink.

Grooming

Beagles are naturally clean. But a beagle cannot stay clean if its living area is dirty. Its bed and blanket should be washed often. If its area is kept clean, a beagle seldom needs a bath. Regular brushing is usually enough to help a beagle stay clean.

A beagle's nails should be trimmed if they get too long. Once a week, its teeth should be cleaned with dog toothpaste. The beagle's long ears also need special care. Its ears should be cleaned once a month. A veterinarian can show a dog owner how to do these things. A veterinarian is a person trained and qualified to treat the sicknesses and injuries of animals.

A beagle's long ears need special care.

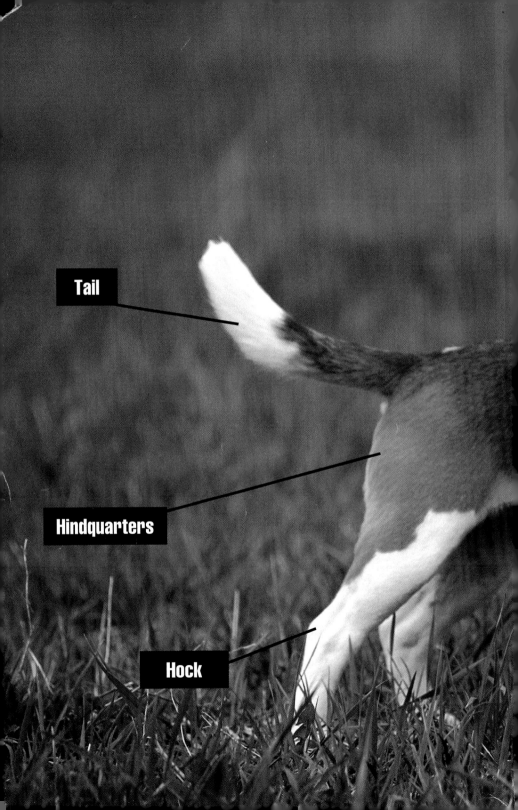

Tail

Hindquarters

Hock

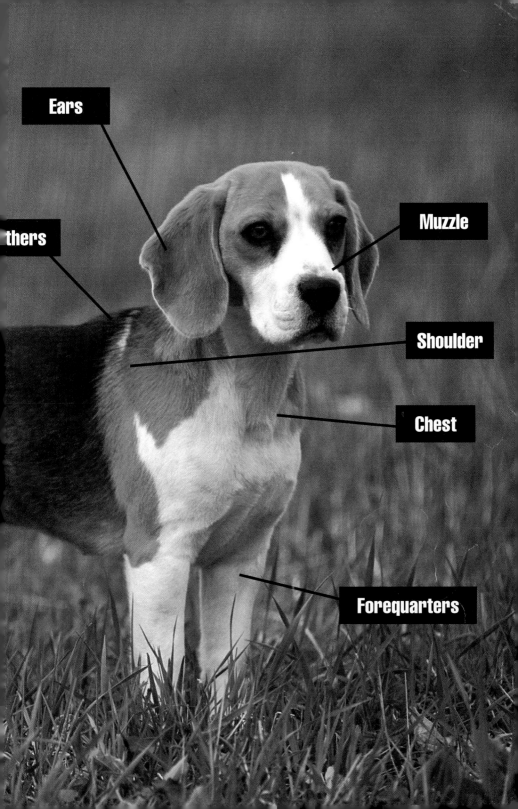

Ears

thers

Muzzle

Shoulder

Chest

Forequarters

Health Care

Dogs need shots every year to protect them from serious illnesses. They need pills to protect them from heartworms. A heartworm is a tiny worm carried by mosquitoes that enters a dog's heart and slowly destroys it. Dogs also need a checkup every year for all types of worms.

During warm weather, beagles should be checked every day for ticks. A tick is a small bug that sucks blood. Some ticks carry Lyme disease. This is a serious illness that can cripple an animal or a human. Beagles should be checked often for fleas, lice, and mites. These are tiny insects that live on a dog's skin.

Finding a Beagle

People looking for beagle puppies can contact beagle clubs to find good breeders. Those wanting a grown dog should ask about rescue shelters. A rescue shelter finds homes for dogs that were abandoned. These dogs cost less than one bought from a breeder. Some are even free.

Whether it is a puppy or an adult dog, a beagle needs a lot of love. With good care, beagles will give that love back.

People looking for beagle puppies can contact beagle clubs to find good breeders.

Quick Facts about Dogs

Dog Terms

A male dog is called a dog. A female dog is known as a bitch. A young dog is a puppy until it is one year old. A newborn puppy is a whelp until it no longer depends on its mother's milk. A family of puppies born at one time is called a litter.

Life History

Origin:	All dogs, wolves, coyotes, and dingoes descended from a single wolflike species. Dogs have been friends of humans since earliest times.
Types:	There are many colors, shapes, and sizes of dogs. Full-grown dogs weigh from two pounds (one kilogram) to more than 200 pounds (90 kilograms). They are from six inches (15 centimeters) to three feet (90 centimeters) tall. They can have thick hair or almost no hair, long or short legs, and many types of ears, faces, and tails. There are about 350 different dog breeds in the world.
Reproductive life:	Dogs mature at six to 18 months. Puppies are born two months after breeding. A female can have two litters per year. An average litter is three to six puppies, but litters of 15 or more are possible.
Development:	Puppies are born blind and deaf. Their ears and eyes open at one to two weeks. They try to walk at about two weeks. At three weeks, their teeth begin to come in.

Life span:	Dogs are fully grown at two years. If well cared for, they may live up to 15 years.

The Dog's Super Senses

Smell:	Dogs have a sense of smell many times stronger than a human's. Dogs use their sensitive noses even more than their eyes and ears. They recognize people, animals, and objects just by smelling them. Sometimes they recognize them from long distances or for days afterward.
Hearing:	Dogs hear better than humans. Not only can dogs hear things from farther away, they can hear high-pitched sounds people cannot.
Sight:	Dogs are probably color-blind. Some scientists think dogs can see some colors. Others think dogs see everything in black and white. Dogs can see twice as wide around them as humans can because their eyes are on the sides of their heads.
Touch:	Dogs enjoy being petted more than almost any other animal. They can feel vibrations like an approaching train or an earthquake about to happen.
Taste:	Dogs do not taste much. This is partly because their sense of smell is so strong that it overpowers their taste. It is also because they swallow their food too quickly to taste it well.
Navigation:	Dogs can often find their way through crowded streets or across miles of wilderness without any guidance. This is a special dog ability that scientists do not fully understand.

Words to Know

brace (BRAYSS)—a pair of dogs that are shown or work together
field trial (FEELD TRYE-uhl)—an event where hunting dogs are judged on their ability to find and retrieve game
game (GAME)—wild animals and birds that are hunted
heartworm (HART-wurm)—a tiny worm carried by mosquitoes that enters a dog's heart and slowly destroys it
kennel (KEN-uhl)—a place where dogs are kept
kibble (KIB-buhl)—dry dog food
Lyme disease (LIME duh-ZEEZ)—a sickness carried by ticks that can cripple an animal or a human
register (REJ-uh-stur)—to record a dog's breeding records with an official club
veterinarian (vet-ur-uh-NER-ee-uhn)— a person trained and qualified to treat the sicknesses and injuries of animals
withers (WITH-urs)—the top of an animal's shoulders

To Learn More

Alderton, David. *Dogs*. New York: Dorling Kindersley, 1993.

American Kennel Club. *The Complete Dog Book*. New York: Macmillan Publishing Company, 1992.

Musladin, Judith, A.C. Musladin, and Ada Lueke. *The New Beagle*. New York: Howell Book House, 1990.

Roth, Richard. *The Beagle: An Owner's Guide to a Happy, Healthy Pet*. New York: Howell Book House, 1996.

You can read articles about beagles in *AKC Gazette, Better Beagling, Dog Fancy, Dog World, Hounds and Hunting, The Rabbit Hunter,* and *Small Pack Option.*

Useful Addresses

American Beagle Club
P.O. Box 121
Essex, VT 05451

American Kennel Club
5580 Centerview Drive
Raleigh, NC 27606

American Rabbit Hound Association
P.O. Box 244
Hoskinston, KY 40844-0244

Canadian Kennel Club
100-89 Skyway Avenue
Etobicoke, ON M9W 6R4
Canada

National Beagle Club
2555 Pennsylvania NW
Washington, DC 20037

Internet Sites

American Kennel Club
http://www.akc.org

Beagles on the Web
http://gabdoc.gdb.org/~laurie/beagles.html

Canine Connections
http://www.cheta.net

Pet Net
http://www.petnet.com

World Wide Woof
http://www.worldwoof.com

Index